Creating a Safe Coaching Environment

sports coach UK is the brand name of The National Coaching Foundation and has been such since April 2001.

ISBN 1 902523 74 1

Authors
Paul Hackett and Shenagh Hackett (Top Lodge Leisure Limited)

Editor
Nicola Craine

Sub-editors
Heather Douglas, Helen Bushell

Designer
Saima Nazir

sports coach UK would like to thank Peter Whitlam (Education Consultant) for his valuable input into this resource.

Photographs courtesy of actionplus sports images

sports coach UK
114 Cardigan Road
Headingley
Leeds LS6 3BJ
Tel: 0113-274 4802 Fax: 0113-275 5019
Email: coaching@sportscoachuk.org
Website: www.sportscoachuk.org

Patron: HRH The Princess Royal

Published on behalf of **sports coach UK** by
Coachwise Business Solutions
Coachwise Ltd
Chelsea Close
Off Amberley Road
Armley
Leeds LS12 4HP
Tel: 0113-231 1310 Fax: 0113-231 9606
Email: enquiries@coachwisesolutions.co.uk
Website: www.coachwisesolutions.co.uk

Preface

Health and safety is an evolving subject. Anyone involved in a specific legal conflict should seek the best legal advice they can. Health and safety resources, such as this one, may not be top of the list of preferred reading material for coaches, employers and deployers of coaches, and development officers. However, we live in a society that has started to develop worrying tendencies:

- We are becoming more likely to sue each other (compensation culture).

- Individuals are becoming more reluctant to accept responsibility for their own actions (blame culture).

- The rights and wrongs of court cases sometimes appear to be less relevant than the depth of the pockets of the defendants or their insurers.

- Many insurers are now settling claims out of court, rather than going to the expense of a full civil hearing.

Many individuals and organisations live in fear of being sued for negligence. If society continues to become increasingly litigious, some will inevitably become victims of this trend. Following the guidelines below can help to reduce the potential of being sued for negligence:

- Managing risk is best for your performers.

- The best defence is a good attack.

- Be proactive about health and safety rather than trying to protect against being sued (eg good practice avoids litigation).

- Helping people to perform safely will reduce the likelihood of litigation.

Most sports have an inherent risk of injury that must be accepted by performers if they are to enjoy the full benefits of participation. This inherent risk should not be used as an excuse to do little or nothing. Providing a safe environment that maximises the benefits and minimises the risks to performers requires all those within the coaching industry to review their practices on a regular basis. All coaches, employers and deployers of coaches, and national governing bodies (NGBs) should review their own guidelines and risk management processes on a regular basis – every two years or when an event occurs which causes risk control measures to be questioned.

This pack is a practical guide to health and safety, and risk management in coaching. It supports the **sports coach UK (scUK)** *Creating a Safe Coaching Environment* workshop and is also designed to be used as a stand-alone resource. It will provide coaches of all levels, employers and deployers of coaches with adequate background knowledge to help them ensure a safe coaching environment. It is not intended to be a definitive guide to health and safety, nor a substitute for professional legal advice. In addition to following the guidance in this pack, all coaches at all levels should adhere to the **scUK** *Code of Conduct for Sports Coaches*[1] or NGB equivalent.

It is impossible to cover all situations and all sports. For some, the guidance provided will be too detailed for the risks involved in their sport; for other more hazardous sports, additional measures may need to be considered. In these circumstances, further advice should be sought from **scUK** and/or the relevant NGB.

The subject of child abuse is deliberately avoided. For guidance on child protection issues, you are recommended to attend the **scUK** *Good Practice and Child Protection* workshop and to read the associated resource *Protecting Children: A Guide for Sportspeople*.

By the end of this pack, you should be able to:

- identify the foundations of good practice risk management in coaching

- recognise and challenge poor health and safety practices – both your own and those of employers and deployers of coaches

- identify appropriate action to take if a lack of health and safety is apparent in an area, facility or activity

- advise performers, parents and guardians about the perceived and actual risks present in the sports in which they are involved

- recognise the roles and responsibilities of other agencies and organisations

- understand the relationship between hazard and risk in a coaching context

- understand that risk is a function of the likelihood and frequency of events occurring

- identify specific hazards to which coaches are exposed

- identify specific action that coaches can take to reduce the likelihood and/or frequency of unacceptable risk.

You may benefit from discussing the guidance provided with colleagues or fellow coaches to share ideas and clarify any issues that may arise. If you identify any hazards for which adequate control measures are not in place, or you feel that you or your performers are at risk, do not hesitate to contact your line manager or NGB for additional guidance.

---

1 Available from Coachwise 1st4sport (tel 0113-201 555 or visit www.1st4sport.com).

Key to symbols used in the text	
	Activity
	Stop and consider
	Important information
	Points of interest
	Remember

Throughout this pack:

- the term *coach* is used to describe anyone involved in leading or delivering sports programmes (eg coaches, leaders, teachers, instructors, development officers, officials, administrators, volunteers, parents/carers) and those with responsibility for the organisation of sport (eg national governing bodies, local authorities, centre managers, sports clubs).

- the term *employers and deployers of coaches* is used to describe organisations or individuals that employ (ie formally pay for) coaches (eg schools, local authorities and leisure facilities) or deploy (ie ask for but do not pay) coaches (eg sports clubs).

- the content complies with Government legislation and is correct at the time of going to print. However, **scUK** cannot be held responsible for omitting any subsequent changes to the law.

- the pronouns *he*, *she*, *him*, *her* and so on are interchangeable and intended to be inclusive of both males and females. It is important in sport, as elsewhere, that both genders have equal status and opportunities.

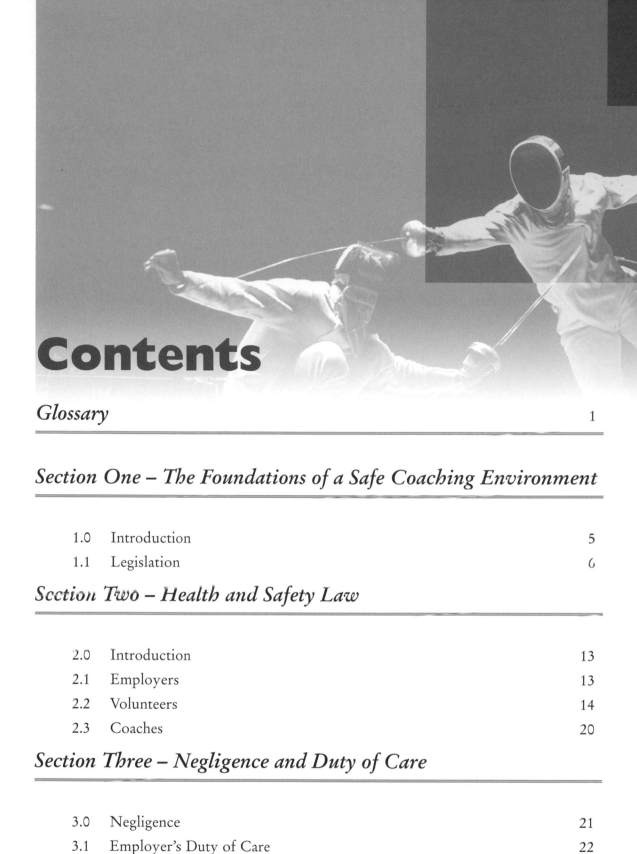

Contents

Glossary 1

Section One – The Foundations of a Safe Coaching Environment

1.0   Introduction   5
1.1   Legislation   6

Section Two – Health and Safety Law

2.0   Introduction   13
2.1   Employers   13
2.2   Volunteers   14
2.3   Coaches   20

Section Three – Negligence and Duty of Care

3.0   Negligence   21
3.1   Employer's Duty of Care   22
3.2   The Common Duty of Care   22

Contents

Section Four – Risk Assessment

4.0	Introduction	31
4.1	Key Terms	32
4.2	Risk Assessment Systems	35
4.3	Severity Ratings	36
4.4	Likelihood Ratings	37
4.5	Events and Outcomes	37
4.6	Common Sense	38
4.7	Assessing Risk	39
4.8	Risk Control	46
4.9	Conclusion	47

Section Five – Summary

5.0	Introduction	49
5.1	Policy	50
5.2	Organisation	51
5.3	Planning	51
5.4	Measuring Performance	52
5.5	Auditing and Reviewing Performance	52
5.6	The Role of Coaches	53

Appendices

Appendix A	Sample Letter to Prospective Performers	55
Appendix B	Sample Physical Activity Readiness Questionnaire (PARQ)	57
Appendix C	Sample Risk Assessment Issues	61
Appendix D	Integrated Risk Assessment Form	75
Appendix E	Accident Reporting	77
Appendix F	Criminal Records Bureau – Guidelines	81
Appendix G	Further Reading	85
Appendix H	**sports coach UK** Contacts	87
Appendix I	Other Useful Contacts	89

Glossary

Acronyms

ACoP	Approved Code of Practice
ALARP	As Low As is Reasonably Practicable
COSHH	Control of Substances Hazardous to Health Regulations
HASAWA	Health and Safety at Work etc Act 1974
HSC	Health and Safety Commission
HSE	Health and Safety Executive
MHSWR	Management of Health and Safety at Work Regulations
PPER	Personal Protective Equipment Regulations
PUWER	Provision and Use of Work Equipment Regulations
RIDDOR	Reporting of Injuries, Diseases and Dangerous Occurrences Regulations
WRULD	Work-related Upper Limb Disorder

Terms

Accident	An undesired circumstance(s), which gives rise to ill health, injury, damage, production losses or increased liabilities. (HSG 65)
Act of Parliament/Statute	Statutory code voted in by both Houses of Parliament, which implements Government policy on behaviour.
Appointed Person	A person who is not a first aider but is appointed and trained by an employer to carry out duties involved in the management of a first aid emergency.
Assessed Risk	A level of risk (of a particular outcome) as valued by expert opinion and based on relevant data, knowledge and experience and most probable conclusions.
Attitude	A predisposition to think, act or feel in a particular way about a particular issue.
Audit/Safety Audit	A systematic and critical examination of each area of an organisation's activity, the object of which is to reduce accidents and minimise loss. The process looks at activity and how well it is carried out.
Breach of Statutory Duty	A criminal offence, but one for which an injured person may make a civil claim if they have suffered injury as a result of the breach, unless specifically excluded by the statute.
Case Law/Judicial Precedent	Authoritative references of previous judicial decisions and interpretations, which assist the subsequent and consistent adjudication of cases. A decision by one court that due to the seniority of that court will apply to all lower courts.
Civil Law	Law that confers rights on individuals and allows redress against the wrongdoer subject to a level of proof in the balance of probabilities. Persons who breach civil law are sued by their fellow citizens.
Civil Liability	Liability in civil law for harm or wrong done to an individual.
Claimant	Replaced the word *plaintiff* as the description of the person pursuing a claim under civil law.
Common Law	A source of law not written in statute but developed over time by judicial precedent.
Compensation	A monetary award given to the victim of a civil wrong, which varies according to the degree of harm done.
Competent Person	A person who has sufficient training or expertise or knowledge or other qualities to be able to assist the employer in the discharge of his statutory duties. (MHSAWR)
Contributory Negligence	Consideration given to the behaviour of an injured person, which determines a proportion of blame and causes damages to be reduced accordingly.
Crime	A breach of criminal law, subject to proof at level as beyond reasonable doubt.
Criminal Law	Branch of law setting out society standards for behaviour and conferring penalties for non-compliance. Persons who breach criminal law are prosecuted by the state.
Damage	The loss outcome of an accident.
Damages	An award of compensation, which is related to the amount of harm done.
Danger	The inherent nature of a thing to do harm.
Defendant	The accused person defending a claim under civil law or a prosecution under criminal law.
Duty of Care	Common law duty placed on all persons to exercise reasonable care that their acts or omissions do not harm their neighbour.

EHO	Environmental Health Officer: an enforcement officer employed by local authorities who has jurisdiction over non-industrial employment, such as sports and sports development, if the local authority does not provide them.
First Aid	Treatment for the purpose of saving life and minimising the consequences of injury until medical assistance is available. It also includes the treatment of minor injuries that may not need medical assistance.
First Aider	A person designated by the employer and trained to the HSE approved level.
Hazard	An exposed danger. Something with the potential to cause harm.
Improvement Notice	Statutory notice issued by a HSE or EHO official when a breach of statute is discovered. A time limit of 21 days is given to comply or appeal to an industrial tribunal.
Indictable Offence	A criminal offence for which high penalties or terms of imprisonment may be applied.
Loss	The net summation of damage and personal injury resulting from an accident.
Major Injury	An injury that is reportable under RIDDOR.
Negligence	*The omission to do something which a reasonable man, guided upon those considerations which ordinarily regulate the conduct of human affairs, would do, or doing something which a prudent reasonable man would not do.* Blythe v Birmingham Waterworks, 1856
(As Far as is) Practicable	A strict duty in which the cost is not a factor. Something is practicable if it is possible to accomplish with known means or resources and feasible within the scope of current knowledge and invention.
Prohibition Notice	A statutory notice issued by an EHO or HSE inspector that requires the recipient to cease or not begin an activity. This notice will be issued when an inspector is of the opinion that the activity presents a risk of serious injury. A breach of statute is not required and the enforcement notice stays in place even if an appeal is lodged.
Prosecute	The act of initiating and pursuing a legal action before the criminal courts.
Reactive Monitoring	An activity directed towards detecting and analysing failures in an organisation's occupational health and safety management system.
Reasonable Care	The common law standard of care expected by the reasonable man.
Reasonable Man	The description given to the hypothetical being who is neither overcautious nor imprudent.
Reasonably Practicable	The legal standard that was defined in case law by Edwards v NCB 1949, where the quantum of risk involved is placed upon one scale and the cost of the measures necessary for averting the risk are placed on the other. Where the costs outweigh the risks involved it is not reasonably practicable to do more.
Regulation or Statutory Instrument	A statutory device approved by Parliament made under a general provision in an Act of Parliament, sometimes called subordinate or delegated legislation. Regulations are not usually qualified by the term reasonably practicable.
Risk	The likelihood that a specific undesired event will occur due to the realisation of a hazard. (HSG 65)
Risk Assessment	The process of identifying and evaluating risks associated with the exposure to a particular hazard. Required under the Management of Health and Safety at Work Regulations. (MHSWR)

Statute Law	Predominately legislation that creates criminal breaches, exceptions include the occupiers Liability Acts 57 and 84, which give rights in civil law only.
Tolerable Risk	The level of risk that is deliberately accepted for the benefit gained by running the risk.
Unacceptable Risk	A risk that is not tolerable.
Unsafe Act	Unsatisfactory behaviour that leads to an accident event. For example, horseplay or not working to NGB standards.
Unsafe Conditions	An unsatisfactory physical condition existing in the workplace, which is significant in leading to an accident event.

Section One

The Foundations of a Safe Coaching Environment

1.0 Introduction

Coaching sport can be a very fulfilling occupation, profession or hobby. However, whenever we undertake to coach sport, we also undertake to accept a range of responsibilities.

Employers and deployers of coaches have a duty to ensure the safety of their coaches as employees. This duty extends equally to full-time professionals, part-time coaches and unpaid volunteer coaches. It involves ensuring coaches' safety while working with performers, possibly by themselves and possibly in relatively inhospitable environments in rural backwaters or on inner-city estates. Coaches are expected to work in a range of environments from warm, comfortable sports centres to disused car parks. They may also be expected to work alone and, in some cases, may drive considerable distances to reach their place of work. Employers and deployers of coaches have a statutory and common law responsibility to ensure that, as far as is reasonably practicable, coaches can carry out their professional duties without being exposed to unnecessary risk.

Employers and deployers of coaches not only recruit professional and volunteer coaches, but may also arrange coaching facilities for them. School halls, school gyms, playing fields, community halls, sports centres, swimming pools and athletics tracks are the most common types of facilities, but many other types may be used on a regular or ad hoc basis. How safe are those premises? Are they suitable for coaches to do their job? Has the owner or occupier carried out a suitable and sufficient risk assessment of the premises and the activities that are to be undertaken within them?

Coaches are responsible for minimising the risk of physical or mental injury to their performers or anyone else affected by their work. They should be aware of the nature of their chosen sport(s) and the varying degree of risk involved for individual performers. They need to be competent to ensure the safety of their performers. They also need to be proactive about safety and be able to deal with the accidents that inevitably occur while coaching and developing a performer or team

Try to identify potential dangers that may exist:

- within the areas in which you coach or ask coaches to work
- while carrying out coaching duties
- while carrying out sport-related activities.

What could you do to minimise the dangers to yourself, your coaches or performers?

Try to identify your best example of how you have reduced risk in your working environment.

1.1 Legislation

Activity 1 provides an introduction to health and safety law.

ACTIVITY 1

Read through the scenarios described in the left-hand column of the table below. In each case, decide if an offence has been committed. If it has, decide if it is covered by criminal law, civil law or both. Then state where you think that law stems from. The first four have been completed for you.

	Scenario	Criminal	Civil	Source of Law
1	Employing a coach who regularly encourages performers to overtrain	*Health And Safety At Work etc Act 1974 (HASAWA)*	*Negligence*	*HASAWA and possibly negligence*
2	Failing to ensure premises are reasonably safe for performers or coaches in a sports facility	*HASAWA 1974*	*Duty of care*	*Possibly Occupiers' Liability Act 1957*
3	Urinating in an alleyway on the way home from the pub	*Yes. Indecent exposure and possibly career-threatening*		*Rehabilitation of Offenders Act Sex Offenders Register*
4	Allowing the music used during floor routines at a gym club to be heard by the neighbours at the sports centre	*Environmental Protection Act 1990 (EPA)*	*Nuisance*	• *Possible noise pollution causing a nuisance to neighbours* • *EPA 1990* • *Would be the same for floodlights*

6

	Scenario	Criminal	Civil	Source of Law
5	Working with a coach who uses hazardous training techniques			
6	A performer discovering that they have an illness which has been made worse by a workout regime recommended to him a few months earlier by a strength and conditioning coach			
7	Locking a belligerent performer in an office			
8	Knowingly allowing a coach or performer to encounter a hazard and potentially come to harm in a sports facility			
9	Failing to report an incident where an employed coach is sent to hospital and kept in overnight for observation			
10	Allowing a coach to use out-of-date and faulty equipment			

Now turn over.

Feedback

Scenario	Criminal	Civil	Source of Law
1	*Health And Safety At Work etc Act 1974 (HASAWA)*	*Negligence*	*HASAWA and possibly negligence*
2	*HASAWA 1974*	*Duty of care*	*Possibly Occupiers' Liability Act 1957*
3	*Yes and possibly career-threatening*	*–*	• *Rehabilitation of Offenders Act* • *Sex Offenders Register* • *Indecent exposure?*
4	*Environmental Protection Act 1990 (EPA)*	*Nuisance*	• *Possible noise pollution causing a nuisance to neighbours* • *EPA* • *Would be the same for floodlights*
5	*Yes*	*Possible negligence as an individual*	• *HASAWA, Section 3* • *Vicarious liability for employees' actions*
6	*Unlikely*	*Negligence*	• *Possible negligence if coach had not made sufficient effort to identify any medical conditions* • *Possible vicarious liability if coach employed by an organisation* • *No offence if Pre-activity Readiness Questionnaire (PARQ) completed and/or performer lied*
7	*Criminal offence committed by the imprisoner*	*–*	*Unlawful imprisonment*
8	*HASAWA*	*Occupiers' Liability Act*	*Criminal source of law dependent on consequences*
9	*Criminal offence subject to possible £5000 fine*	*–*	*Reporting of Injuries, Diseases and Dangerous Occurrences Regulations (RIDDOR) (Details are contained in Appendix F)*
10	*Possible criminal offence*	*Possible claim for damages*	• *HASAWA and Provision and Use of Work Equipment Regulations (PUWER)* • *Probable lack of risk assessment* • *Management of Health and Safety at Work Regulations, Regulation 3 (MHSAW)*

	Scenario	Criminal	Civil	Source of Law
11	Not providing an employed coach with wet weather gear and expecting him to work in the rain			
12	A coach (person) is involved in a serious car crash while driving between two sessions that she runs for a local authority sports development unit			
13	An athlete is aiming for a personal best in the pole vault, despite the fact that the competition has already been won, the light is starting to fade and the track manager has made it clear it is unsafe to continue. The officials, the athlete and her coach choose to ignore the track manager and continue. The athlete is injured after misjudging her landing			
14	A coach is overseeing his team practising basic skills. He is informed that he has an important phone call in the main building and leaves the squad session to take the call. While he is absent, one of his performers is injured			
15	A rugby coach returns to the sport after a ten-year break. He teaches the game as he was taught and has always taught it. During a training session, a player is injured using a technique that is not currently approved for her age group			

Now turn over.

Feedback

Scenario	Criminal	Civil	Source of Law
11	• *HASAWA* • *Personal Protective Equipment Regulations (PPER)*	*Unlikely to have civil consequences*	*An employer has a duty to assess workplace risks (including wet, hot, cold or exposure to excess sunshine) and provide adequate personal protective equipment*
12	• *Road Traffic legislation*	*Vicarious liability*	*The coach may have committed a road driving offence and may be dealt with by the police. However, any damages caused by the accident may be the responsibility of his employer who is vicariously responsible for his actions while carrying out his normal duties*
13	• *HASAWA*	*Occupiers' Liability Act 57, contributary negligence*	*This is a complex case that involves a number of people who may be jointly and severally liable under the HASAWA (civil negligence and contributory negligence by the athlete). There is no one right answer – a case like this would be decided according to the circumstances. The track manager may be guilty of an offence under the HASAWA. A negligence claim could potentially be made against the coach, the track manager's employer and the officials, and, if the athlete received compensation, it would probably be reduced by 50–100% for contributory negligence (ie when a person contributes to the harm or loss they suffer due to their own actions)*
14		*Negligence Vicarious liability*	*The coach would probably be considered to be negligent. The club, school or employer or deployer of the coach may also be considered negligent (vicarious liability)*
15		*Negligence Vicarious liability*	*The coach would probably be considered to be negligent. The club, school or employer or deployer of the coach may also be considered negligent for not ensuring that their employee was up to date with current knowledge or practice*

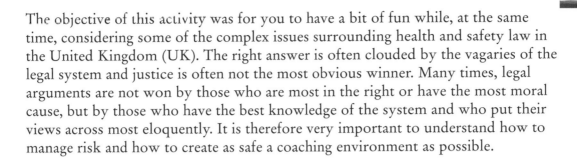

The objective of this activity was for you to have a bit of fun while, at the same time, considering some of the complex issues surrounding health and safety law in the United Kingdom (UK). The right answer is often clouded by the vagaries of the legal system and justice is often not the most obvious winner. Many times, legal arguments are not won by those who are most in the right or have the most moral cause, but by those who have the best knowledge of the system and who put their views across most eloquently. It is therefore very important to understand how to manage risk and how to create as safe a coaching environment as possible.

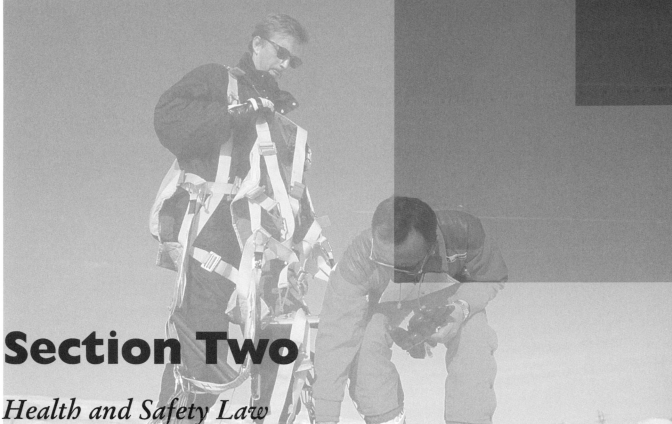

Section Two

Health and Safety Law

2.0 Introduction

Health and safety law consists of a large, complex range of regulations and statutes. The aim of this section is not to provide an in-depth review of all of these, but to outline key issues.

2.1 Employers

Employers need to be aware of the legal implications of the Health and Safety at Work etc Act 1974 (HASAWA) and the duties it imposes on them to ensure the safety of their employees in their place of work, wherever that may be. The Act also requires employers to ensure the safety of subcontractors and performers who are affected by their work. As far as is reasonably practicable, employers need to provide:

- a safe place of work with adequate welfare facilities

- safe equipment

- safe systems of work

- safe access and egress from work

- suitable supervision

- competent fellow employees

- sufficient training, instruction and information to enable employees to carry out their work properly.

The various regulations enacted under the auspices of the HASAWA are used to provide detailed guidance on various safety issues. The key regulations which apply to employers and deployers of coaches include:

- Health and Safety (First Aid) Regulations
- Management of Health and Safety at Work Regulations
- Workplace Health and Safety Regulations
- Provision and Use of Work Equipment Regulations
- Manual Handling Regulations
- Reporting of Injuries, Diseases and Dangerous Occurrences Regulations (RIDDOR).

2.2 Volunteers

Without the volunteers who manage the majority of sports activities in the UK, we would be in a very sorry state. Most clubs rely on volunteers to enable their activities to run. Varying degrees of risk are associated with these activities, all of which need to be assessed. In this resource, the term *employer and deployer of coaches* is used.

When a coach is an employee of an organisation that is asking them to coach, the legal position is very clear. When the employer/deployer of coaches is a club with one or more employees, the position is relatively clear. However, when the club consists of an informal association of like-minded people, the relationship between the coach and the constitution of the club becomes less clear. In these circumstances, if an incident occurred, the ensuing case would need to be decided in accordance with the facts surrounding it.

The degree of control and authority that employers/deployers can exercise over volunteer coaches is usually less than in a direct employment situation. Getting volunteers to comply with health and safety regulations is a challenge for sports clubs and relies on cooperation rather than compulsion. It is therefore essential that members of club management set appropriate standards and convince volunteers to adhere to them.

Legal Issues

Clubs with at least one part-time employee are covered under the terms of the HASAWA. Volunteer coaches are not considered to be employees; however, under Section 3 of the HASAWA, employers are required to carry out their duties in such a way as to ensure the safety of people other than employees as far as is reasonably practicable. In addition, the Management of Health and Safety at Work Regulations (1999) place a duty on employers to assess the risks to employees and anyone who may be affected by their activities. The risks identified should be adequately controlled.

When young people are used as volunteer coaches, risk assessments should take into account their relative inexperience, lack of awareness of risks and immaturity. Coaches should be selected for their suitability for the task, rather than just because they are available.

Clubs with no paid employees are covered purely by civil law. A coach could sue the employer/deployer of a volunteer coach if he was injured by the activities he undertook for and on behalf of the club. In addition, a performer or her legal guardian could sue if the performer was injured as a result of a negligent action committed by a volunteer coach (this risk applies to all coaches). In most cases, the club and the coach would be sued for negligence and the club and/or the coach would usually hold public liability insurance which would cover the cost of the claim. However, the subsequent publicity and increased insurance premiums could affect the viability of the club's and coach's future.

The majority of other regulations do not apply to volunteers and personal protective equipment does not therefore need to be issued. However, relevant risk assessments, in which personal protective equipment is recommended as an appropriate control measure, should be shared with volunteer coaches to encourage them to dress appropriately.

Health and Safety Law

Assume that you are a representative of an employer or deployer of coaches who is responsible for the management of coaching programmes. Read through each scenario in the table below and, in the right-hand column, note how you think each one could best be handled and what the best proactive solution would be.

	Scenario	Your Thoughts
1	You have just appointed a community racket sports coach to deliver existing coaching programmes. She has coaching qualifications in badminton, tennis and squash. The role requires her to travel the length and breadth of the county to various locations. What measures could you take to verify that she is a suitable and competent coach?	
2	An established coach with 20 years' experience has routinely run programmes in one part of the county. You have transferred him to another programme that has been running well for the last five years. The performances and standards of the new performers in his charge have recently deteriorated and attendance has dropped significantly. What issues need to be considered?	
3	Over the last 12 months, a few performers have suffered serious injuries at a facility that you use for weights and resistance training. They were all under the supervision of the same coach.	

	Scenario	Your Thoughts
4	While on a social visit to a facility, you notice a trampoline session being run by one of your coaches, but cannot see the coach present in the hall. The session is in full flow and the performers appear to be enjoying themselves. The coach is in the reception area talking to a parent. You ask one of the other parents about the session and they say that the coach is very rarely there until the session has been running for 20 minutes.	
5	During an altercation at the end of an activity, a performer injures one of your coaches. The performer in question is known to be volatile and has caused problems on previous occasions.	
6	You hire a school hall in which to run a coaching programme. The school's staff set up gymnastics and trampolining equipment in the hall and leave it out until your coach arrives. At the end of each coaching session, the coach leaves the equipment out for the school staff to store away. One evening, a young person gains access to the hall after the session has finished and your coach has departed. Unfortunately, the trespasser is injured on the equipment.	

Now turn over.

Feedback

Employers/deployers should not rely on national governing body (NGB) qualifications alone – they should check the competence of coaches for themselves. Examples of good practice relating to the previous activity are provided below. Some of these may already be in place within your coaching environment. If they are not, consider how they could be introduced.

Scenario 1

As a manager of coaching programmes, you should ensure that:

- the employer and deployer of coaches has a driving policy

- coaches have an orientation or induction before commencing their role

- coaches are monitored by supervisors and managers on a regular basis (more regularly at the start of employment; less often later on when they are more established) to ensure that standards are in line with NGB expectations

- the appropriateness of the structure, content and style of coaching programmes is assessed, taking into account the level of the sessions within it

- coaches produce activity plans

- the quality and content of activity plans are scrutinised frequently

- coaches produce progress reports on activities, both on a formal and informal basis

- coaches produce written procedures for important areas of the activities

- you have completed a Criminal Records Bureau (CRB) check on all coaches (see Appendix F for further details)

- coaches have appropriate insurance.

Scenario 2

The feedback to Scenario 1 also applies here. In addition, as a manager of coaching programmes, you should ensure that:

- the coach has maintained Continuing Professional Development (CPD) over the last few years and is using the most appropriate methods

- coaches produce routine reports on activities and that the information supplied in those reports is acted upon by line managers

- line managers meet regularly with coaches, both via formal appraisals and more informal situations, and that trusting relationships develop between managers and coaches.

Scenario 3

As a manager of coaching programmes, you should:

- investigate all injuries and ill health incidents that occur during coaching programmes
- develop an incident/accident trend analysis
- ensure that all performers wear appropriate clothing and footwear
- ensure that a first aid kit is available which is suitable for treating anticipated sports and soft tissue injuries
- monitor standards and develop action plans to reverse reduced performance or improve current performance
- ensure that all coaches are qualified in first aid at a level appropriate to the sports they are coaching
- ensure that performers are suitably mentally and physically prepared for the activity they are taking part in
- check facilities for undue risk and appropriateness of equipment for the activities being undertaken
- review the risk assessments of host facilities
- carry out regular checks on the facilities in which coaches are expected to work to ensure continued safety.

Scenario 4

As a manager of coaching programmes, you should:

- carry out regular observations, moderations, evaluations or verification visits to ensure that standards of coaching are being maintained
- ensure that all coaches undergo frequent professional development and work to the highest standards
- ensure that coaches are paid to prepare and set up their activities, and to be present at the start of the warm-up to ensure safety (unless appropriately qualified assistance is present)
- audit coaching policy, standards and performance measures
- ensure that line managers carry out regular safety inspections of premises used
- develop a safety reporting procedure based on audits and inspections.

Scenario 5

As a manager of coaching programmes, you should ensure that:

- performers are expected to sign up to a performance contract
- coaches are empowered to exclude any group or individual for misbehaviour
- coaches are provided with adequate support if performers misbehave or are likely to be a problem (eg not working alone)
- performer/coach ratios are in line with NGB guidelines
- coaches are not required to coach in locations that pose an exceptionally high

risk of physical assault (if a particular group of performers is a high priority, coaching sessions should be located in a safe place and the performers brought to the coach).

Scenario 6

As a manager of coaching programmes, you should ensure that:

- all dangerous equipment is made safe at the end of each session (ie stored in a safe place)

- security is such that it is difficult for intruders to gain access to the facility

- no-one is exposed to known hazards – not even intruders (as per Occupiers' Liability Act 1984 requirements).

Responsibility for the intruder's injury would depend on who was responsible for securing the facility and storing the equipment.

The aim of this activity was to get you to think about the management of coaches. Employers and deployers of coaches are responsible for the actions of their employees, contractors, self-employed people and volunteers. This concept is known as *vicarious liability*.

Employers and deployers of coaches also have a duty of care towards their coaches to ensure that, as far as is reasonably practicable, working conditions are free of unnecessary risk.

Coaches expect to be respected. Employer and deployers of coaches must ensure that all those working for them are properly supervised and carry out their duties. This can be a difficult line to tread, but even the most able and motivated people need the comfort of managerial concern and support.

Occupiers of buildings have a duty of care to their legitimate visitors and a lesser duty of common humanity to trespassers under the Occupiers' Liability Act 1984. A facility should be left in a safe and secure condition at the end of every day, especially if it is foreseeable that it may be subject to vandalism. Employers and deployers of coaches have a duty to ensure that the facilities and equipment their coaches are expected to use are suitable and fit for purpose.

2.3 Coaches

Coaches also need to be aware of the HSAWA. As employees, coaches are responsible for taking reasonable care of their own health and safety, and that of others who may be affected by their acts or omissions. They must also cooperate with their employers to effect health and safety.

Self-employed coaches have the same duties as employers and employees, but are not required to provide documented health and safety policies.

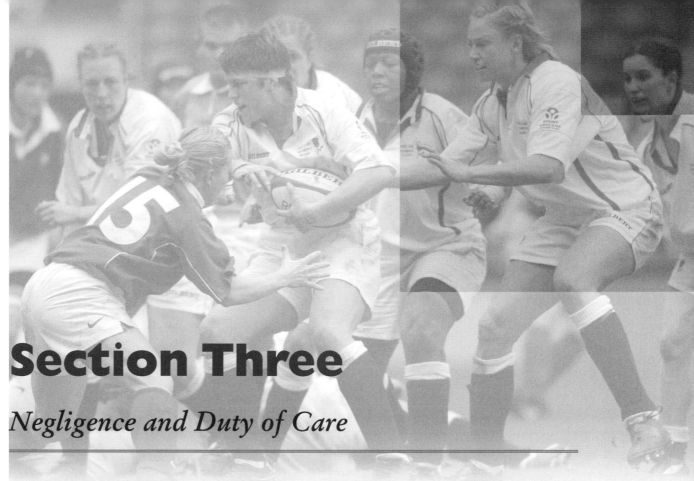

Section Three

Negligence and Duty of Care

3.0 Negligence

Negligence can be defined as *careless conduct causing injury or loss to another*. In order for a civil claim for damages on the grounds of negligence to be successful:

- a duty of care must have been owed to the injured party
- that duty of care must have been breached
- damage, loss or injury must have resulted from, or been caused by, that breach.

The usual legal defences against negligence are listed below:

- **Voluntary assumption of risk**
  The injured party is willing and therefore no harm can be done to him. For example, a performer in a sporting event may get injured as a direct result of participation. However, no claim could be made as injuries are part and parcel of sport, especially contact sports.

- **Contributory negligence**
  The injured party is partially responsible for her own injuries. For example, a cyclist, who is hurt as a result of a collision with a car during a cycle race on a public road, may be considered to be partially liable for her own actions, assuming that she contributed to the collision. Therefore, any compensation won may be reduced by a certain percentage to take into account her proportion of the responsibility. If the cyclist had no lights or reflective jacket, the reduction would be higher; if she had followed all safety precautions, it would be lower.

- **Due diligence**
  All that could be done to prevent harm being done had been done. In most cases, a suitable and sufficient risk assessment with completed action plan would be the first and most important step to demonstrate due diligence.

All of these concepts would be subject to legal testing in a court of law.

3.1 Employer's Duty of Care

Under common law, employers have a general duty of care towards their employees (including contractors and volunteers acting as employees). Employers must take reasonable care to protect their employees from the risks of foreseeable injury, disease or death at work. If employers know, or in the light of current knowledge should know, of a health and safety risk or hazard, they will be liable if one of their employees is killed or injured or suffers an illness as a result of the risk, or if they failed to take reasonable care to avoid this happening. Employers should therefore carry out risk assessments of coaches' work and workplaces.

Vicarious Liability

Employers and deployers of coaches are held responsible in law if, in the course of their employment, one of their employees negligently injures another person. The employers and deployers of coaches would usually be sued for negligence in these circumstances, not the employee. Although, at first glance, this may seem unfair to employers and deployers of coaches, it is because they are deemed to be in control of their employees.

For example, if a coach driving recklessly between coaching sessions had an accident that led to a performer, who was a passenger in the car, being injured, the police would prosecute the driver of the vehicle for the road traffic offence. The performer or her legal guardian would have the right to sue the employer or deployer of the coach if the coach was continuously employed. However, if the coach was a sessional coach, the employer or deployer may not have a legal responsibility for travel undertaken by the coach between coaching sessions.

Criminal acts on the road are the responsibility of the individual, while civil wrongs are the responsibility of the employer or deployer of the coach.

3.2 The Common Duty of Care

The common duty of care is a duty to take such care as in all the circumstances of the case is reasonable, to see that the visitor (performer, coach or other person) will be reasonably safe in using the premises (or area) for the purposes for which he is invited or permitted by the occupier to be there.

This definition of the common duty of care is derived from the Occupiers' Liability Act 1957. This Act deals with the issue of risk being willingly accepted and allows for risk to be accepted by performers while participating in their sport. Spectators are covered by the common duty of care but are required to accept a degree of risk which it would be unreasonable to eliminate.

The Occupiers' Liability Act 1957 also deals with the issue of children:

An occupier must be prepared for children to be less careful than adults.

An occupier must also assume a greater responsibility for children and vulnerable adults.

Coaches therefore need to ensure that:

- they take more care over the health and safety of children and vulnerable adults who may not appreciate risk

- adult performers and parents of child performers are aware of the risks that they are exposed to while being coached or participating in a sport.

It can therefore be concluded that employers and deployers of coaches have a duty of care for coaches, regardless of the form of their employment or voluntary service.

Coaches also have a duty of care for their performers, whatever their age or ability. They have a higher duty of care for less able and younger performers.

Trespassers

The Occupiers' Liability Act 1984 created a duty of care to trespassers – a duty of common humanity. Trespassers should not be exposed to a known risk without making reasonable attempts to prevent them from coming into contact with them. This puts the onus on those in control of facilities to ensure that dangerous equipment or other known hazards are left in a secure condition at the end of coaching session. This is especially important if it is reasonable to assume that trespassers may be expected.

ACTIVITY 3

1   As an employer or deployer of coaches, what best practice control measures can you use to reduce the potential of a claim of negligence being made against your organisation by:

•   coaches?

•   performers?

2   As a coach, how can you use best practice to reduce the potential of being sued for negligence as an individual by one or more of your performers?

Now turn over.

Feedback

Scenario 1

Examples of good practice relating to Scenario 1 are provided below:

- Employers and deployers of coaches should firstly check NGB qualifications and then references. Once satisfied that coaches are suitable, their competence should be checked via direct observation.

- Coaches should be vetted via the Criminal Records Bureau (CRB).

- Coaches should be monitored by supervisors and managers on a regular basis to ensure that the structure, content and style of their coaching is in line with NGB expectations.

- Coaches' workplaces should be inspected on a regular basis by supervisors and managers.

- Coaches should produce activity plans for each session.

- The content and quality of activity plans should be scrutinised frequently.

- Coaches should produce progress reports on activities.

- Coaches should be punctual – they should be paid for time before and after sessions to ensure their prompt arrival.

- Coaches should produce written procedures for important areas of activities.

- Coaches should have an emergency contact number for their employer/deployer.

- Coaches should be empowered to exclude difficult or uncooperative performers.

- Employers and deployers of coaches should expect coaches to behave in a reasonable and professional manner and should reciprocate by doing so themselves.

- Assessors should be sent to coaching facilities before they are used.

- Employers and deployers of coaches should request sight of risk assessments before permitting coaches to work on site.

- Appropriate contracts should be drawn up with coaching facilities.

- Facilities should be checked to ensure that they comply with the terms of the contract.

- On-site support and contacts should be clearly defined (eg access to telephone, cooperation of on-site staff).

- Coaches should be empowered to delay or cancel activities if safety is in doubt (eg frozen pitch, water on court from leaking roof, algae in open water).

- Coaches should be trained to carry out on-site risk assessments.

- Coaches should have access to first aid kits if they are not available at their coaching venue and have the skills, and be willing, to use them.

- If facilities cannot/will not supply adequate means of communication, coaches should have access to mobile phones and have the skills, and be willing, to use them.

- Responsible adults should be provided if facilities cannot/will not supply support staff to observe activities.

- Emergency action plans should be developed to deal with foreseeable incidents which may arise at each venue.

- Coaches should be provided with contact numbers for caretakers, head teachers or facility managers to ensure that safe access and egress is maintained.

- Alternative venues/waiting areas used before and after sessions should be agreed in advance.

- Procedures should be in place to enable coaches to report to their employer/deployer if they find a facility is unsuitable.

Scenario 2

Examples of good practice relating to Scenario 2 are provided below:

Coaching Issues

- Plan your activity properly and ensure appropriate progression throughout the season.

- Evaluate the performers' physical and skill levels.

- Write your training plans down and keep them safe.

- Do not deviate from the plans without good reason. **If you do need to deviate, note the reason.**

- Be as up to date as possible with current practice in your sport.

- Coach within the accepted norms of your sport and the abilities of your performers.

- Be clear and consistent with your performers, and give adequate feedback.

- Only delegate coaching tasks to competent people and ensure that you stay in control.

- Check the coaching area for hazards and remove or avoid them.

- Keep control of your performers.

- Develop a checklist for the facilities you use.

- Make prudent judgements about continuing if conditions become more hazardous (eg inclement weather).

- Use the most appropriate equipment for the intended activity.

- Teach your performers how to use equipment and how to wear kit properly.

- Inspect all equipment on a regular basis. Repair or take out of use damaged equipment.

- Give written instructions to performers (and their parents if necessary) to support verbal instructions.

- Ensure that performers who are involved in contact activities are matched in terms of maturity, size and skill.

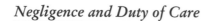

- Play to the rules and modify sessions to account for individual skill levels.

- Ensure that your performers are physically ready for the intended activity – possibly via a PARQ. (See example in Appendix B.)

- Keep medical notes on file for your performers and seek medical advice before letting injured or recovering performers participate fully.*

- Stay in control of all activities and be prepared to take action to prevent injury.

- Know your sport so well that you anticipate all foreseeable injuries and, where possible, be in a position to prevent them.

- Prohibit reckless behaviour.

- Pay more attention when developing new skills.

- Warn performers and parents of the inherent risks of the sport you are coaching (possibly in writing). Remind performers about these risks as appropriate, taking into account the age of the performers and the activity they will be involved in. (See example of letter in Appendix A.)

- Always carry a first aid kit and be proficient in its use. (First aid qualifications should be backed up with sport-specific knowledge and training.)

- Ensure that your first aid kit is suitable for treating anticipated sports and soft tissue injuries.

- Prevent injuries by ensuring that your performers wear appropriate kit and equipment.

- Be prepared to carry out first aid up to, and including, cardiopulmonary resuscitation (CPR).

- Ensure that blood and other body fluid spills are mopped up using disposable cloths and that the affected areas are disinfected with a mild bleaching solution. The cloths should be disposed of as contaminated waste. Disposable gloves should be used.

- Ensure that all records are kept in a secure place.

---

*   Ensure that notes containing private information are kept in a secure manner in line with the Data Protection Act 1998.

Professional Behaviour

The following examples of professional behaviour relate to both scenarios 1 and 2:

- Where possible, ensure that you have at least one witness to your actions at all times.

- Do not work alone in situations where accusations of poor practice are possible.

- Follow written procedures provided by employers and deployers of coaches, NGB guidelines and the *scUK* Code of Conduct for Sports Coaches[1].

- When coaching young performers, try not to place yourself in a situation where an accusation could be made and where independent witnesses could not help you refute them[2].

- Maintain professional relationships with your performers.

- Keep physical contact to an essential minimum to assist the development of a skill or required stature.

- Ensure that you have access to a telephone (mobile or landline) at the site at which you are working.

- If you rely on a mobile phone, ensure that a signal is available at the site at which you are working, that the phone is fully charged and that you know the full address of the venue in case you need to inform the emergency services.

- Ensure you are familiar with access routes for emergency services.

- Be aware of, and follow, any emergency procedures that are in place at the venue.

- Have an emergency plan for each facility you use.

Summary of Issues Presented in Scenarios 1 and 2

- Be proactive about health and safety rather than trying to protect yourself against being sued.

- Helping people to perform safely will reduce the likelihood of litigation.

- Managing risk is best for your performers.

- The best defence is good and safe practice.

---

1 Available from Coachwise 1st4sport (tel 0113-201 5555 or visit www.1st4sport.com).

2 For further guidance, refer to **scUK**'s *Protecting Children* resource, which is available from Coachwise 1st4sport (tel 0113-201 5555 or visit www.1st4sport.com).

Section Four

Risk Assessment

4.0 Introduction

A risk assessment establishes the likelihood of injury or loss to performers, coaches, volunteers, employers of coaches and others who may be affected by their work, by examining the arrangements in place to control significant hazards.

The key word in the context of risk assessment is *significant*. A sensible approach to risk assessment should be adopted – it can be all too easy to go to unnecessary extremes.

ACTIVITY 4

Try to think of a number of reasons why risk assessment could be criticised and note these in the space provided below:

Now turn over.

31

Feedback

Common criticisms of risk assessment include the following:

- Stopping at assessment with no controls in place.

- It is seen as a paper exercise with little or no value. The same effort is devoted to a hazard such as losing a hairgrip, as to taking up the wrong position for a tackle in a contact sport such as rugby (ie concentrating on the insignificant to the detriment of the significant).

- It may be allocated to the most junior (or least competent) person in the group who knows the least about best coaching practice or other industry guidelines. This demonstrates the importance of risk assessment in the eyes of senior management and, consequently, its importance to the rest of the organisation.

- Hours of effort are put into re-writing established industry guidelines when much of the good practice is already documented. In this case, all that is necessary is to demonstrate that existing controls are in place.

- It is over-complicated by consultants who try to turn it into a pseudo-science.

- It is used as an excuse to prevent activity, rather than to enhance it by enabling it to be carried out with less risk.

- It is reduced to ticking boxes and organising files, rather than a thought-provoking process which enables things to be done better.

- It is a bureaucratic process that offers no benefit to organisations or their coaches.

- It is a way of preventing people from doing their job the way they have always done it.

If the focus is on significant issues, not trivialities, and control measures enhance safety while enabling activities to continue, the process of risk assessment should make coaching a more efficient and fun pastime for both coaches and performers. Developing coaching protocols and method statements for tasks results in normal operating procedures (NOPs[1]), which can be used as a basis for inductions and training. Risk assessments should also highlight areas that may lead to emergency situations so that these can be anticipated and action plans developed to deal with them. Risk assessments and emergency action plans[2] are a requirement for employers and deployers of coaches and the self-employed under the terms of Regulation 8 of the Management of Health and Safety at Work Regulations 1999 (EAPs[2]).

4.1 Key Terms

The key terms associated with risk assessment include the following:

Hazard   Something that has the potential to cause harm.

Risk   A function of how likely something is to happen set against the most probable severity if it did happen.

Likelihood   The probability that the potential hazard will come to fruition, taking into account the control measures that are in place.

Severity   The harm or loss that the hazard has the potential to cause.

1 Normal Operating Procedures (NOPs) – the documented day-to-day procedures for operating a facility.

2 Emergency Action Plans (EAPs) – the documented procedures implemented to deal with foreseeable emergencies.

ACTIVITY 5

1 In the space provided below, list what you consider to be the most serious hazards for coaches in the context of the tasks they perform, the areas they perform them in and the activities they are involved in. List a maximum of seven hazards in each category.

Tasks

Areas

Activities

2   In the space provided below, list what you consider to be the seven most serious hazards facing employers and deployers of coaches in the context of the tasks they perform, the areas they perform them in and the activities they are involved in.

Tasks

Areas

Activities

4.2 Risk Assessment Systems

Many of the risk assessment systems which are commercially available only assess the risk of injuries to either the employee or a member of public. In the context of coaching, it is also important to consider the effect an incident could have on a coach's reputation, thus preventing him from working for many years.

The risk assessment system outlined in this section consists of three areas of assessment:

- **People** – injuries

- **Assets** – equipment and facilities

- **Reputation** – media coverage and damage to an individual's or organisation's ability to carry out their role in light of public acceptance.

There are three possible outcomes:

High Risk	Control measures must be developed for this activity to continue. Method statements should be developed to cover the significant aspects of the programme, activity or facility. These method statements would then form the basis of a training plan that would be used to induct coaches into the programme.
As Low As is Reasonably Practicable (ALARP)	The control measures and method statements that are currently in place are suitable and sufficient for the activity to proceed safely. However, every effort should be made to ensure that all control measures remain in place.
Low Risk	No further assessment of this is necessary, unless something happens to change either the likelihood or severity.

No matter what risk assessment system is used, the process is essentially subjective. There is no one right way of assessing risk. However, it is generally believed that no one person should be left to carry out the task alone. Risk assessments are best carried out using a team approach. The team should include someone who is experienced in assessing risk and who fully understands the techniques selected. The team should also include one or more people who are familiar with the subject or activity area being assessed and, preferably, someone who is not particularly familiar. Adopting a team approach tends to even out the bias of over-familiarity and naivety.

4.3 Severity Ratings

Severity ratings can be altered to suit the size and complexity of the organisation being assessed. What is catastrophic for a small, independent company providing coaches to a local authority may well only be critical or marginal to the local authority.

In order to make a judgement of the severity of an event, use the tables below to help interpret the outcome.

Table 1: Severity ratings

Severity	People	Assets	Reputation
Catastrophic 4	Multiple fatalities or permanent disabilities.	Extensive damage. Equipment written off or facilities destroyed beyond economical repair. Replacement required.	• Loss of reputation leading to inability to practice • NGB ban for life
Severe 3	Fatality or permanent or long-term disability.	Major damage. Specialist repair required. Out of use until repaired.	• Most performers go elsewhere for coaching • NGB suspension
Critical 2	Major injuries leading to loss of work or training time for three or more days.	Damage. Repairable locally but out of use until then.	• Only the most loyal performers stay with you • NGB disciplinary hearing
Marginal 1	Minor injuries. First aid is sufficient. No time off competition or work.	Minor damage. Self-repair possible but out of use.	• A few performers go elsewhere • NGB formal warning
Negligible	Slight injuries. No first aid required. No loss of training or work.	Minor damage. Repairable and usable in current condition.	• No one leaves, but a few quips are made about your standards • NGB informal warning

4.4 Likelihood Ratings

In order to judge the likelihood of an event happening, use the table below:

Table 2: Likelihood ratings

0	Improbable	So unlikely as to be nearly impossible – no events in living memory
1	Remote	Unlikely in most circumstances but has happened
2	Occasional	Could occur sometime and has been known to occur
3	Probable	Will happen to someone in the industry this year
4	Frequent	Will definitely happen or has happened recently

4.5 Events and Outcomes

Events which result in undesired occurrences are often described as *accidents*. Figure 1 below demonstrates that an *incident* or *accident* is the result of an *event* which can lead to a number of *outcomes*. For this reason, such events are often referred to as *hazardous events*.

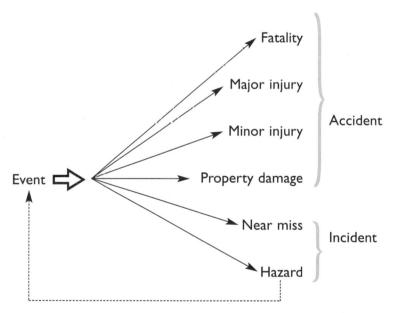

Figure 1: Events and outcomes [1]

The outcome of an event varies mainly as a result of luck, together with, to a lesser or greater extent, the existence of workplace precautions. For example, once a javelin has been thrown, it can result in any of the outcomes shown in Figure 1. However, if everyone on the track is standing in a safe area (an NOP for athletics arenas), the likelihood of the javelin causing a fatality is significantly reduced. However, throwing a javelin will always create a hazard.

---

[1] Based on an original diagram in *Managing Safely* by the Institution of Occupational Safety and Health (IOSH). Reproduced with the kind permission of IOSH.

4.6 Common Sense

Standing in a safe area when javelins are being thrown may be considered common sense to an athletics coach, but it may not occur to a young performer, who has just finished a 100-metre sprint, to do so.

Leaving things to common sense is always difficult because common sense does not really exist. All people have is a limited perception of risk from their viewpoint. What is obvious to one person may not be obvious to another who has a different perspective.

ACTIVITY 6

What do you see when you look at the image below?

• An old woman with a hook nose and a shawl?

or

• A fashionably dressed, demure young woman with a petite nose?

Now turn over.

Feedback

Whichever you see, you are right because they are both there. Your perceptions will lead you to one view or the other. However, with some effort you will be able to see both aspects of the image.

As a risk assessor, you will be able to train yourself to have an open mind to risks – even those with which you are so familiar that you may not even appreciate they are there.

4.7 Assessing Risk

ACTIVITY 7a

Using the risk matrix on page 41, refer back to the hazards you identified in Activity 5 (see page 33) and try to rank them in order of seriousness in the table below.

Hazards for Coaches
Hazardous tasks
Hazardous activities
Hazardous areas

ACTIVITY 7b

Hazards for Employers and Deployers of Coaches

Hazardous tasks

Hazardous activities

Hazardous areas

Table 3: Risk matrix

Severity				Likelihood				
Rating	People	Assets	Reputation	Improbable 0	Remote 1	Occasional 2	Probable 3	Frequent 4
Catastrophic 4	Multiple fatalities or permanent total disability.	Extensive damage. Write-off and needs to be replaced.	Catastrophic impact. Expulsion by NGB.	High risk A				
Severe 3	Single fatality or permanent total disability.	Major damage.	Major impact. Suspension by NGB.					
Critical 2	Major injury or health effects.	Damage.	Considerable impact. Disciplinary by NGB.		ALARP B			
Marginal 1	Minor injury or health effects.	Minor damage.	Minor impact. Formal warning by NGB.					
Negligible 0	Slight injury or health effects.	Slight damage. Self-repair possible. Unsightly but useable.	Slight impact. Informal warning by NGB.	Low risk C				

ACTIVITY 8

Look at the most serious hazard listed in Activity 7a (ie high-risk activities, tasks or areas) and try to identify how you could lower the risk by either reducing the likelihood of that hazard occurring or reducing the severity of the impact should it occur. Some examples of ways to reduce risk are listed below:

- Coaches could reduce the frequency of full-contact matches during training for younger performers to reduce the frequency of impact injuries, or they could require performers to wear protective guards during specific training sessions to reduce the effect of impact.

- Coaches could follow guidelines outlined in their NGB coaching manuals.

- Employers and deployers of coaches could improve coaching standards by initiating regular auditing of coaching programmes.

Note your suggested risk control measures in the space provided below:

ACTIVITY 9

Look back at the control measures you identified in Activity 7 and consider whether they are currently in place within your own coaching practice. Is anyone or anything at risk if they are always rigorously applied? If they are not applied, why aren't they? Complete the table below.

What is the Risk? What is the Most Likely Outcome?	Control Measure	In Place Now Y/N	Rigorously Applied Y/N	Why are the Control Measures not Applied Rigorously?
Impact injuries	Reduce full-contact matches during training for younger performers			Coach believes that match play develops skills and stamina better
Impact injuries	Require performers to wear protective guards such as shin guards and gumshields			Performers cannot afford shin pads or gumshields

ACTIVITY 10

Use the information obtained from the previous activities and your own coaching practice to complete the form below. Column one should be completed from Activity 7. Identify who is at risk in column 2. Column 3 identifies what controls are in place, such as working to NGB standards. Column 4 is used to identify what else could be done to improve safety. The further action column will be used in Activity 11.

Hazard and Risk	Group(s) at Risk	Controls in Place	Further Action Required

ACTIVITY 11

Look back at the *Further Action Required* column in Activity 10 (page 44) and the panel on page 2. Consider who should be responsible for implementing these further control measures and what needs to be done to implement them. Then try to give an estimated date by which the control measures could be implemented. Complete the table below.

Area	Action to be Taken	Responsiblity Of	Review Date	Completion Date

Feedback

The action plan is the most important part of the risk assessment process. Making a list of the hazards and controls only indicates that an organisation is aware of the risks it faces. However, a series of completed action plans with updated risk assessments demonstrates proactive safety management.

A range of risk assessment hazards and controls is contained in Appendix C.

4.8 Risk Control

Employers and Deployers of Coaches

One of the key issues facing NGBs and employers and deployers of coaches is the maintenance of the standards set during initial training and the CPD of their coaches. In every profession, there is a continuum of employees with varying levels of skill and ability. Coaches will vary from the very best, whose standards are exemplary, to the worst, whose standards are very poor. Employers and deployers of coaches need to identify coaches at both extremes of the continuum without disrupting the work of the best.

All employers and deployers of coaches need a system of control. The main methods of control are described in the good practice feedback to Activity 3 (see page 26).

Risk assessment should be reviewed at least every two years or when something happens to alter the judgement that has been made. This may include an accident or incident that calls your judgement into question.

Active Monitoring

In order to meet their legal duties, employers and deployers of coaches need to proactively monitor their employees and volunteers. This enables them to monitor activities and respond before performance begins to deteriorate. Proactive monitoring involves:

- producing routine reports
- examining documents
- carrying out systematic inspections
- monitoring environmental factors, including weather conditions
- monitoring performers' health
- observing behaviour
- carrying out audits
- producing safety reports for relevant personnel
- carrying out risk assessments.

Reactive Monitoring

Reactive monitoring is less effective, but easier to carry out. It involves reacting to events such as:

- injuries and ill health
- property and other losses
- incident analysis
- reduced performance standards
- accidents.

Coaches

For guidance on risk control measures, coaches are recommended to consult:

- NGB guidelines
- scUK's *Code of Conduct for Sports Coaches*[1]
- scUK's *How to Coach Sports Safely* booklet[1].

4.9 Conclusion

Good employers and deployers of coaches use a mixture of monitoring and control techniques. Risk assessment involves more than collating a number of activities, tasks or facilities, and allocating them a numerical value. The essence of risk assessment is formulating a plan of action (a risk reduction plan) to make the working conditions of staff, performers and others safer and more productive.

1 Available from Coachwise 1st4sport (tel 0113-201 5555 or visit www.1st4sport.com).

Section Five

Summary

5.0 Introduction

Figure 2 on page 50 provides a useful summary of the key elements of health and safety management. Each element is explained in further detail in subsequent subsections.

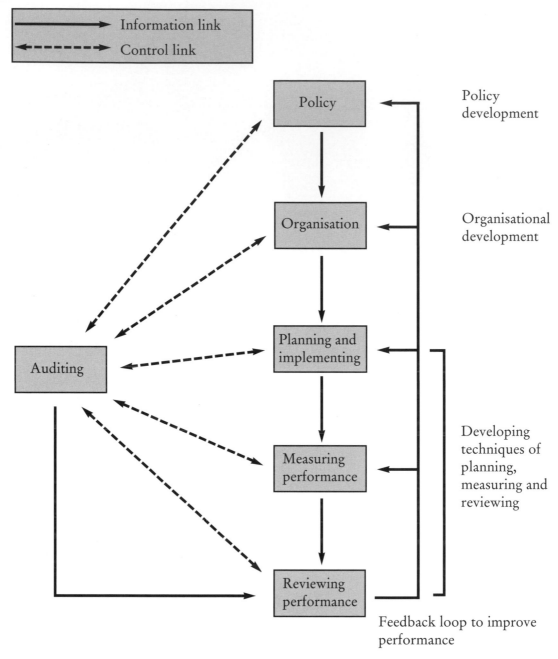

Figure 2: Key elements of health and safety management[1]

5.1 Policy

The starting point for any organisation is to produce an effective health and safety policy. Apart from being a legal requirement, this is good management practice. An effective health and safety policy sets a clear direction for the organisation to follow. It contributes to all aspects of the organisation's performance and demonstrates a commitment to continuous performance. Responsibilities to coaches, performers and others are met in ways which fulfil the spirit and letter of the law.

---

[1] Based on an original diagram in Health and Safety Executive HS (G) 65: Successful Health and Safety Management (ISBN 0 717612 76 7). Crown copyright material is reproduced with the permission of the Controller of HMSO and Queen's Printer for Scotland.

5.2 Organisation

An organisation needs to have an effective management structure and arrangements in place to deliver the health and safety policy. All coaches should be motivated and empowered to work safely, and to protect their own and their performers' long-term health, not simply to avoid accidents.

These arrangements need to be:

- underpinned by the involvement of coaches and performers in health and safety issues

- sustained by effective communication and the promotion of competence, which allows coaches to make responsible, informed and positive contributions to health and safety.

When a shared, common understanding of the organisation's vision, values and beliefs exists, with visible and active leadership by managers, employers and deployers of coaches can foster a positive environment in which health and safety can flourish.

The structures and processes used should:

- establish and maintain management control of the coaching organisation

- promote cooperation between individual coaches, other groups and host venues so that safety is a collaborative effort

- ensure the communication of necessary information throughout the organisation

- ensure that coaches are suitably competent to carry out their work for the organisation.

5.3 Planning

Health and safety policies can only be implemented if a planned and systematic approach to the management of coaching is adopted. Key issues to consider include the following:

- The overall aim should be to minimise risks.

- Risk assessment methods should be used to set priorities and objectives for eliminating hazards and reducing risks that coaches and performers may be exposed to.

- Choosing adequate facilities for the activities to be delivered should minimise risks.

- Appropriate equipment and coaching methods should be used.

- When coaching many sports, it is impossible to eliminate all risk. Therefore, risk should be minimised by using the best physical control measures available. If written instructions and protocols are relied on as a system of control, they will inevitably fail as human nature leads to mistakes or forgetfulness. When a system fails, it will lead to a rapid reduction in safety standards.

- Performance standards for coaches should be established and used as a means of measuring performance. Senior managers should promote a positive health and safety culture.

The above list of good practice strategies should be considered in conjunction with the examples of good practice provided on pages 8, 10, 18–19 and 26–29.

5.4 Measuring Performance

The performance of coaches should be measured against agreed standards, so that the need for improvement can be identified. Employers and deployers of coaches should monitor how effectively health and safety is functioning by checking facilities, equipment, coaches, performers, procedures and systems. Control measures introduced as a result of risk assessments may fail to prevent events occurring. However, reactive monitoring (eg accident investigation, ill-health monitoring) should help to discover why the events occurred.

The objectives of active and reactive monitoring are to:

- determine the immediate causes of sub-standard performance
- identify any underlying causes and implications for the management of health and safety.

5.5 Auditing and Reviewing Performance

All employers and deployers of coaches should try to learn from all relevant past experiences and take appropriate action. This is best carried out as a systematic review of performance based on data obtained from monitoring and independent audits of health and safety systems. These may be internal or external audits, depending on the complexity of the organisation.

Audits should assess:

- legislative compliance
- best practice guidance from authoritative bodies such as NGBs
- compliance with own health and safety policy
- risk control measures.

Performance should be assessed by:

- reference to internal performance indicators
- comparisons with similar organisations and other best practice organisations.

5.6 The Role of Coaches

Coaches can influence health and safety by:

- planning the activities they deliver effectively

- providing appropriate instruction

- ensuring a safe environment

- providing appropriate, suitable and sufficient equipment

- ensuring that performers are evenly matched in terms of physical and skills-related ability and development

- ensuring that performers are sufficiently physically and mentally prepared to participate in the planned activities

- supervising activities

- identifying inherent risks and providing adequate warnings

- providing suitable and sufficient first aid and emergency cover for the planned activities.

The above list of good practice strategies should be considered in conjunction with the examples of good practice provided on pages 8, 10, 18–19 and 26–29.

Appendix A

Sample Letter to Prospective Performers

Page 56 contains a sample letter to prospective performers.

(insert address)

(insert name)
(insert address)

Dear (*insert name*)

Responsibility for Safety in Sport

You have/your child has expressed an interest in participating in (*insert specific sport*). The potential for injury exists in any sport. As a responsible organisation, we will do our utmost to prevent any injuries but some will inevitably occur. The responsibility for safety in sport is shared among administrators, coaches, trainers and performers. The declaration below is intended to bring to your attention the potential for physical injury and harm, and your responsibility for preventing it. It does not absolve (*insert name of organisation*) from its responsibilities for your/your child's health and safety.

Physical injury includes bumps and bruises, muscle strains, soft tissue injuries and, in exceptional circumstances, bone breaks, which may include serious spinal or head injuries. In very rare cases, deaths have occurred while participating in sport.

For female performers, the risk of injury increases if training leads to a disruption of their menstrual cycle. If this occurs, performers should inform their coach and seek immediate medical advice.

Should you wish to discuss any aspects of this letter further, please contact (*insert name of relevant person*).

Yours sincerely

(*insert name*)

Declaration

* I understand that there is a risk of physical injury when participating in any sport (*or insert specific sport*).

* I undertake to inform my coach of any injury that I receive, either while participating in sport or elsewhere.

* I undertake to seek prompt medical assistance to treat any injury I may receive.

Signature of performer _____ Date _____

Signature of parent/guardian _____ Date _____

Appendix B

Sample Physical Activity Readiness Questionnaire (PARQ)

Name	
Date	
Address	
Contact details	Tel no 1	Tel no 2
Date of birth/age		Gender: Male / Female
Proposed sport or activity	

Note: The information collected on this form will only be used for the purposes of assessing your readiness to participate in sport. It will be secured in a safe place and will be disposed of securely and in an environmentally sensitive way when it becomes invalid or if you ask us to remove it from our systems.

Participating in sport is enjoyable and is good for your health and well-being. Being more active and participating in sport is beneficial for most people. However, some people should check with their doctor before participating in sport or increasing their levels of activity.

Sample Physical Activity Readiness Questionnaire

Please answer the following questions honestly by ticking either the **Yes** or **No** box. If you are under 16, a parent or guardian should countersign the form in the presence of your coach or an other responsible person.

	Yes	No
1 Have you ever been advised by a doctor not to participate in any exercise programme?	☐	☐
2 Do you ever feel pains in your chest or arms when exercising?	☐	☐
3 Do you ever feel pains in your chest or arms when *not* exercising?	☐	☐
4 Do you ever feel giddy, lose your balance for no apparent reason or have blackouts?	☐	☐
5 Are you currently using prescription or non-prescription drugs?	☐	☐
6 Do you suffer from joint or bone problems that get worse after exercise?	☐	☐
7 Do you know of any other reason why you should not participate in exercise?	☐	☐
8 Are there any other medical issues that the coaching team should be made aware of?	☐	☐
9 Are there any religious or cultural issues (eg long periods of fasting) that the coaching team should be made aware of?	☐	☐
10 Are you, or might you be, pregnant?	☐	☐

Now turn over.

If you answered **Yes** to any of the above questions, you should:

- talk to a doctor (or an other appropriately medically qualified person) before undertaking strenuous exercise
- tell them about your answers to the questions above
- tell them what exercise you plan to participate in.

If you have already spoken to an appropriately medically qualified person, you may participate in an appropriate amount of exercise in line with the advice you have been given. Please make sure you share this advice with your coach. It is normal to start slowly and build up your level of exercise over a period of time. Reassess your fitness regularly and inform your coach and medical advisor immediately of any changes.

If your honest answer to all of the questions is **No,** you can be reasonably sure that it is safe to start becoming more active. Begin slowly and build up gradually. Have your fitness tested regularly and adjust your exercise in line with your improving fitness. If you feel unwell, do not participate on that day. If you have an infection, it could become more serious if you become too tired and you may infect your colleagues.

Signature of performer   _____ Date _____

Signature of coach   _____ Date _____

Signature of parent/guardian   _____ Date _____
if performer is under 16

Appendix C

Sample Risk Assessment Issues

Pages 62 to 73 contain a range of sample risk assessment issues for coaches and employers and deployers of coaches.

Risk Assessment Issues for Coaches

Accusation of Improper Behaviour

Hazard and Risk	Groups at Risk	Controls
Accusation	Coaches	• Where possible, ensure you have a witness to your actions. • Do not work alone in situations where accusations are possible. • Follow written procedures from NGB guidelines for employers and deployers of coaches. • When coaching young performers: – never place yourself in a situation where an accusation could be made and independent witnesses could not help you refute them – be aware of the possibility of performers becoming infatuated with you – keep physical contact to an essential minimum to assist the development of a skill or required posture.
Parents do not turn up to collect their child and you are left with him	Coaches	• Get at least one other adult to stay with you, preferably a qualified coach or parent. • Stay in a public place that is well lit, preferably indoors. • Arrange a suitable collection and meeting place in advance. • Have a list of coaches' and parents' telephone numbers to hand. • Notify parents by phone and a follow-up letter that it is irresponsible for them to abandon their children. • Publish coaching session times and stick to them. • Run your sessions for a set amount of time so that parents are trained to collect their children on time. • Encourage parents to arrive early or participate in coaching sessions (subject to CRB checks when available).
Transportation of children to and from sessions	Coaches	• Where possible, always arrange for another independent adult to travel with you. • Children should always travel in the rear of vehicles with their seatbelts fastened. • Only transport children if you have the written agreement of their parents/guardians.

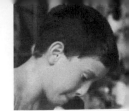

Injury to Coaches and Performers

Hazard and Risk	Groups at Risk	Controls
Injury to self	Coaches	• Always carry a first aid kit and be proficient in its use. (First aid qualifications should be backed up with sport-specific knowledge and training.)
Injury to performers	Performers	• Prevent injuries by ensuring that performers wear appropriate kit and equipment. • Ensure that you have a structured warm-up and progression over time. • Ensure that your first aid kit is suitable and sufficient to treat anticipated sports and soft tissue injuries. • Ensure that you have access to a telephone at the site at which you are working. • If you rely on a mobile phone, ensure that a signal is available and that you have the full address of the venue in case you need to inform the emergency services. • Ensure that you are familiar with access routes for emergency services. • Contact your employer or deployer of coaches. • Contact the premises manager of the site at which you are working. • Be aware of, and follow, any emergency procedures that are in place at the venue. • Mop up blood and other body fluid spills using disposable cloths and disinfect the affected areas with a mild bleaching solution. Dispose of the cloths as contaminated waste. Use disposable gloves.

Stress, Communication and Illness

Hazard and Risk	Groups at Risk	Controls
	Coaches	• Consider keeping your address and home telephone number private. • Consider having a separate business line/mobile phone for coaching activities.
Illness (self before coaching session)	Performers	• Ensure that someone else (possibly two people) goes to the venue you were due to be working at with instructions to ensure the safety of the performers. • This other person/people should not run the session unless they are qualified and competent to do so. • Arrange for the performers to be contacted by phone to inform them that the session has been cancelled.

Working Alone

Hazard and Risk	Groups at Risk	Controls
Attack Physical assault at place of work	Coaches	• Assess the risks present at the venue. • Consider whether the venue poses a greater risk than other suitable venues. • If a more suitable venue is available, use this one instead. • If the threat of physical harm is still present, ensure that adequate support is present to deter troublesome behaviour. • If support is not available or would not be effective, do not use the venue for your coaching session.

Manual Handling

Hazard and Risk	Groups at Risk	Controls
Injury caused by moving equipment	Coaches and performers	• Where possible, arrange for the coaching venue to be set up so that equipment does not need to be handled manually. • If equipment does need moving, try to use suitable trolleys and aids if possible. • Carry out a manual handling risk assessment that includes the following: **Task** – Does the task involve lifting, lowering, twisting, carrying, pushing or dragging? – If so, does moving it create a significant risk of injury to the people involved? **Load** – Is the load abnormally large, heavy, bulky? Does it have handholds or is it unstable? Could it be unduly hot or cold? – If so, does it create a significant risk of injury to the people involved? **Working environment** – Is the working environment hot or very cold? – Is the floor in good condition? – Can the lifter move freely? – Is equipment likely to be affected by gusts of wind? – Is there suitable lighting to enable people to see where they are going? **Individual capacity** – Does moving the equipment require unusual strength or capacity? – Does moving the equipment present a particular risk to anyone who may be pregnant? – Are special skills, ability or knowledge required to erect or dismantle the equipment? – Should young or inexperienced people be supervised?

Risk Assessment Issues for Employers and Deployers of Coaches

Hazard and Risk	Groups at Risk	Controls
Working in schools and other facilities owned by other organisations		• Send assessors to facilities before they are used.
		• Request sight of risk assessments before permitting coaches to work on site.
Coach or employer/deployer of coaches losing reputation for adverse events at subcontracted premises	Employer/ deployer of coaches	• Ensure that appropriate contracts are drawn up with facilities.
		• Check that facilities comply with the terms of the contract.
	Coaches	• Ensure that on-site support and contacts are clearly defined (eg access to telephone, cooperation of on-site staff).
	Performers	• Empower coaches to delay or cancel activities if safety is in doubt (eg frozen pitch, water on court, algae in water).
Performers being injured due to inappropriate facilities		• Train coaches to carry out on-site risk assessments.
		• Provide coaches with first aid kits if none are available at their venue.
		• If facilities cannot/will not supply adequate means of communication, provide coaches with mobile phones.
		• If facilities cannot/will not supply support staff to observe activities, provide assistant coaches.
		• Develop an emergency action plan to deal with foreseeable incidents at each venue.
		• Provide coaches with contact numbers for caretakers, head teachers and managers to ensure that safe access and egress is maintained.
		• Ensure that alternative venues/waiting areas used before and after sessions are agreed in advance.
		• Ensure that procedures are in place to enable coaches to report to their employer/deployer of coaches if they find a facility is unsuitable.

Risk Assessment Issues for Employers and Deployers of Coaches (continued)

Hazard and Risk	Groups at Risk	Controls
Coaches working unsupervised are not maintaining appropriate standards	Employer/deployer of coaches (reputation) Performers (physical or mental harm) Coaches (reputation)	• Do not rely on NGB qualifications alone – check the competence of coaches. • Ensure that coaches are vetted via the CRB. • Arrange for coaches to be monitored by supervisors and managers on a regular basis to ensure that the structure, content and style of their coaching are in line with NGB expectations. • Ensure that coaches' workplaces are inspected on a regular basis by supervisors and managers. • Ensure that coaches produce activity plans for each session. • Ensure that the quality and content of activity plans are scrutinised regularly. • Ensure that coaches produce progress reports on activities. • Ensure that coaches are punctual – pay coaches for time before and after sessions to ensure their prompt arrival. • Ensure that coaches have written procedures for important areas of activities. • Ensure that coaches have an emergency contact number for the duty controller or line manager. • Empower coaches to exclude difficult or uncooperative participants. • Expect coaches to behave in a reasonable and professional manner and reciprocate by acting as a reasonable and professional employer/deployer of coaches.

Risk Assessment Issues for Employers and Deployers of Coaches (continued)

Hazard and Risk	Groups at Risk	Controls
		• Ensure that line managers meet regularly with coaches in an informal/casual context and that they develop trusting relationships.
		• Ensure that coaches produce routine reports on activities and that line managers act upon the information supplied.
		• Ensure that line managers carry out regular safety inspections of premises used.
		• Carry out regular checks of the host establishments' documentation (eg normal operating procedures, standard operating procedures, minimum operating standards NOP/SOP/MOP) and coaches' driving-related documentation.
		• Carry out regular checks of the condition of buildings and areas in which coaching takes place to ensure continued safety.
		• Carry out regular weather checks on open-air activities to ensure that appropriate precautions are being taken and clothing worn, and that activities are brought indoors when required.
	Coaches	• Carry out regular observations, moderations, evaluations or verification visits to ensure that coaching standards are being maintained.
		• Establish policies for coaching activities.
	Employer/ deployer of coaches	• Establish standards and performance measures for coaching activities.
		• Carry out regular audits of coaching policies, standards and performance measures.
	Performers	• Develop safety reporting procedures based on audits and inspections for senior managers.
Insufficient monitoring of coaches leading to loss of standards		• Investigate all injuries and ill health incidents that occur during coaching programmes.
		• Investigate all property loss events.
		• Develop an incident/accident trend analysis.
		• Monitor standards and develop action plans to reverse reduced performance or improve current performance.
		• Ensure that all coaches produce activity plans for their sessions.
		• Ensure that coaches provide appropriate instructions for the performers they are working with.
		• Ensure that coaches have a safe place to work in.
		• Ensure that coaches have suitable equipment for the performers they are working with.
		• Ensure that performers are as evenly matched as possible in terms of physical ability, skill ability and skill development.

Risk Assessment Issues for Employers and Deployers of Coaches (continued)

Hazard and Risk	Groups at Risk	Controls
Accusation of unprofessional activities and poor advice	Employers and deployers of coaches (reputation) Performers (physical or mental harm) Coaches (reputation)	• All coaches and volunteers should be CRB checked. • Coaches should be encouraged to take out suitable professional indemnity insurance. • Employers and deployers of coaches should have compulsory employers' liability insurance. • Employers and deployers of coaches should insist that all employed coaches undergo frequent CPD. • Coaching should be arranged to take place in facilities where coaches are not likely to be left alone with a performer or group of young performers. Chaperone services could be considered. • Coaches should be required to mentor younger coaches and/or attend basic skills refresher courses, especially in sports where coaching techniques have developed over recent years. • When parents do not turn up to collect children, set procedures should be in place with a safe place to wait in public, well-lit areas, which are preferably protected from the weather. • A system of nominating authorised collectors should be arranged. Children should not be released to anyone other than an authorised collector. Children should not be allowed to leave coaching sessions by themselves. • If young performers travel with a coach in a private car, they should sit in the rear of the vehicle. • All coaches should be qualified in first aid. First aid should be administered in the presence of witnesses while maintaining the privacy and dignity of the casualty as far as possible. • Parent volunteers should always be closely supervised. As a general policy, all volunteers should be CRB checked and closely monitored. Unqualified volunteers should not be allowed to be responsible for coaching sessions. • Coaches should be aware of the possibility of young performers becoming infatuated with them, mistaking their attention for a sign of fondness or affection. For some young performers, the attention they receive during coaching sessions may be the most they receive in their lives. • Coaches should only coach up to their level of competence.

Risk Assessment Issues for Employers and Deployers of Coaches (continued)

Hazard and Risk	Groups at Risk	Controls
Injury to performer participating at an unsuitable level	Employers and deployers of coaches (reputation) Performers (physical or mental harm) Coaches (reputation)	• Inform performers and parents/guardians that risk is inherent in all sports. • Ensure that performers are required to complete a PARQ to check they are suitably fit before participating in sport. • Ensure that the level of activity is matched to the skill and physical size of the performers involved. • Ensure that performers are mentally and physically prepared for the intended activity. Specialist assistance should be provided for those who may need additional coaching/help. • When working with disabled performers, coaches should have received adequate manual handling training for specific lifts or manoeuvres. • All coaches should be qualified in first aid. First aid should be administered in the presence of witnesses while maintaining the privacy and dignity of the casualty as far as possible. • Coaches and volunteers should be made aware of any medical conditions their performers may have and of any specific treatment required (eg epi-pens for anaphylactic shock, sugar for diabetics). • The younger the age of the performers, the higher the ratio of coaches to performers should be. The ratio can be lower when working with groups of adults, assuming the risk of violence to the coach is low. • All coaches should be aware of the location of the nearest telephone or mobile phone. • All coaches should be briefed on accident reporting procedures. • All accidents or first aid incidents should be investigated.

Risk Assessment Issues for Employers and Deployers of Coaches (continued)

Hazard and Risk	Groups at Risk	Controls
Injury to coach	Coaches (physical harm)	• Coaches should be empowered to exclude any group or individual for misbehaviour. • Coaches should be provided with adequate support if performers misbehave or are likely to be a problem (ie not working alone). • Performer/coach ratios should be in line with NGB guidelines. • Coaches should not be required to coach in locations that pose an exceptionally high risk of physical assault. If a particular group of performers is a high priority, coaching sessions should be located in a safe place and the performers brought to the coach.
Failure or absence of equipment	Coaches (physical harm) Performers (physical harm)	• Ensure that correct equipment is available to coaches. • Ensure that coaches only use correct equipment via frequent monitoring visits. • Ensure that facilities provide appropriate equipment which is maintained correctly. • Ensure that equipment that is provided is kept in good order and that faulty or obsolete equipment is removed and destroyed or quarantined.
Manual handling of equipment	Coaches Performers	• Ensure that all coaches are familiar with the equipment they are expected to use. • Carry out a risk assessment of the facility with a view to establishing manual handling issues (or train coaches to carry out their own manual handling risk assessments). • Draw up contracts with facility providers which require facilities to be presented in a suitable condition for coaching.

Risk Assessment Issues for Employers and Deployers of Coaches (continued)

Hazard and Risk	Groups at Risk	Controls
Unforeseen cancellation of sessions (eg structural or building fabric failure, power failure)	Coaches Performers	• All young performers must provide contact numbers for their parents/guardians. • Coaches, employers and deployers of coaches should have contact numbers for performers, parents/guardians, schools, leisure centres etc in case they need to contact them in the event of an emergency cancellation. • Coaches should be empowered to relocate or change their sessions in order to ensure safety. • Safe, alternative activities/venues should be agreed in advance.
Vicarious liability for those who are driving during the course of their normal duties on behalf of employers and deployers of coaches	Road traffic users	• Illegal or negligent driving methods should not be condoned (eg the use of mobile phones while driving is prohibited while working for the organisation). • All coaches and staff should stop their vehicle and park safely before accepting or making mobile phone calls. • Fully-fitted, hands-free equipment that automatically answers and disconnects may be used to receive short calls on the move, but must not be used to initiate calls. • All driving licences should be checked on an annual basis. • All vehicle MOTs (if applicable) should be checked on an annual basis. • All vehicle insurance certificates should be checked on an annual basis to ensure that they are valid and cover business use. • All vehicles should carry an appropriate road fund licence. • All coaches and staff must carry a first aid kit in their vehicle at all times when working for the organisation.
Transport accidents or incidents	Performers Coaches Volunteers	• All drivers should be CRB checked. • All vehicles used for transporting performers and coaches should be roadworthy and fully insured. • No vehicle should be overloaded with passengers – there should be no more passengers than usable seatbelts. • All passengers should wear a seatbelt.

Appendix D

Integrated Risk Assessment Form

This risk assessment is in an integrated style that includes all the steps used in the resource on a single page – it should be used in conjunction with the Risk Matrix on page 41.

Name of Facility	Date	Assessor
Activity, Task or Area being Assessed		
Persons at Risk		
Hazards		
Controls in Place		
Severity Level	Likelihood Level	Risk Ranking A B C

Further Controls Required	Action Plan		Action Taken
	Responsiblity	By When	

Reassessment with Additional Controls		
Severity	Likelihood	Risk Ranking A B C
Signature of Assessor	Date Next Assessment Due	

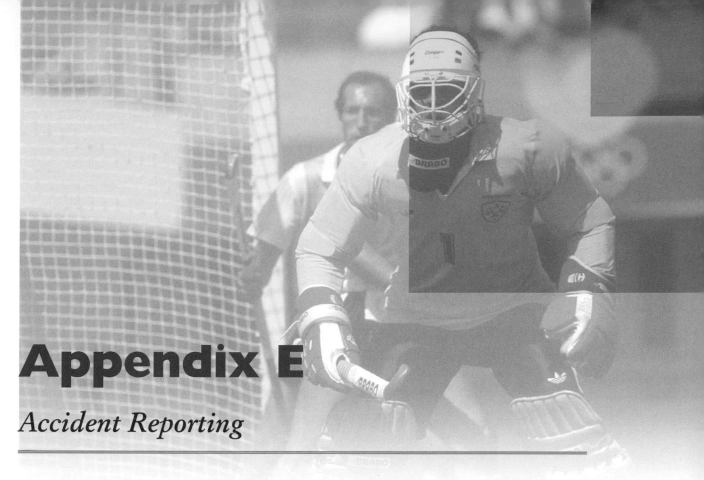

Appendix E

Accident Reporting

The legal basis for accident reporting is contained in a range of regulations and statutes, which include the following:

- Health and Safety at Work etc Act 1974

- Social Security (Claims and Payments) Regulations 1979

- Social Security Administration Act 1992

- Reporting of Injuries, Diseases and Dangerous Occurrences Regulations (RIDDOR) 1995.

This appendix provides a brief outline of these acts and regulations and is not intended to be a definitive guide to the law.

Employees and Volunteers

Employees and volunteers who have an accident while carrying out their coaching duties that results in them being injured or becoming ill, are required to tell their employer/deployer as soon as possible. The best way for them to do this is to complete an accident report or arrange for a colleague to complete it on their behalf. Their employer/deployer should then investigate the incident and, if the injury or illness prevents employees/volunteers from carrying out their duties for three days or more, they should report it to the Health and Safety Executive (HSE). Incidents that could have lead to a serious injury must also be reported to the HSE.

Employed coaches who have to take three or more days off work may receive Statutory Sick Pay (SSP). If they do not qualify for SSP, they may still be entitled to State Incapacity Benefit. If the incident leads to permanent disability, they may be entitled to Disablement Benefit.

By filling in the correct accident forms at the right time, employees and volunteers will protect their potential rights to these benefits.

Employers and Deployers of Coaches

Employers and deployers of coaches must ensure that records of injuries to employees and volunteers are kept. To this end, an accident book should be provided in which employees and volunteers can record details of accidents that lead to injuries. The accident book should be accessible at all times and only one page per person should be used. Completed pages should be removed and stored in a safe place to protect any personal information, as required by data protection law.

Accidents involving performers should also be recorded. However, injuries caused as a direct result of sports participation are not usually considered to be reportable under RIDDOR.

Accident records should be kept for at least three years in the case of adults. Parents of children have until their child is 18 years old to claim, after which the child has a further three years. Therefore, accidents that may have serious consequences should be retained until the victim is 21 years of age.

The self-employed should report accidents and illnesses to themselves in the same way as an employer.

Reporting Procedure under RIDDOR

Fatalities and major injuries must be reported to the HSE immediately. Contact details are provided below:

Tel: 0845-300 9923

Fax: 0845-300 9924

Email: riddor@natbrit.com

Website: www.riddor.gov.uk

A more comprehensive report should be submitted to the HSE on form F2508 within 10 days. Other less serious incidents, such as those that lead to three or more days off work, should also be reported within 10 days. F2508 reports should be sent to the Local Authority Environmental Health Department.

Reportable Injuries

The following major injuries must be reported to HSE:

- fracture of any bone except those in the finger, thumb or toe
- amputation
- dislocation of the shoulder, hip, knee or spine
- temporary or permanent loss of sight
- any penetrating injury to the eye
- electrical shock or burns if this leads to unconsciousness or requires a hospital stay of 24 hours or more

- any other injury that:
  - leads to hypothermia, heat-induced illness or unconsciousness
  - requires resuscitation
  - requires admittance to hospital for 24 hours or more
- acute illness requiring medical attention or unconsciousness caused by chemical substances or biological agents
- any injury that leads to three or more days absence from work, including normal days off
- any physical or physiological injury listed above caused by violence[1].

Reportable Dangerous Occurrences

Reportable dangerous occurrences include a range of equipment failures that could lead to death or serious injury.

Reportable Infections

The following infections may be encountered during coaching and should be reported to the HSE:

- hepatitis
- legionellosis
- leptospirosis
- lyme disease
- tetanus
- tuberculosis
- any other animal-related infections.

---

1 Violence is 'any incident in which an employee or volunteer is abused, threatened or assulted by a member of the public in circumstances arising out of the course of his or her allocated duties'.

When to Report Incidents

The diagram below summarises when incidents should/should not be reported to HSE.

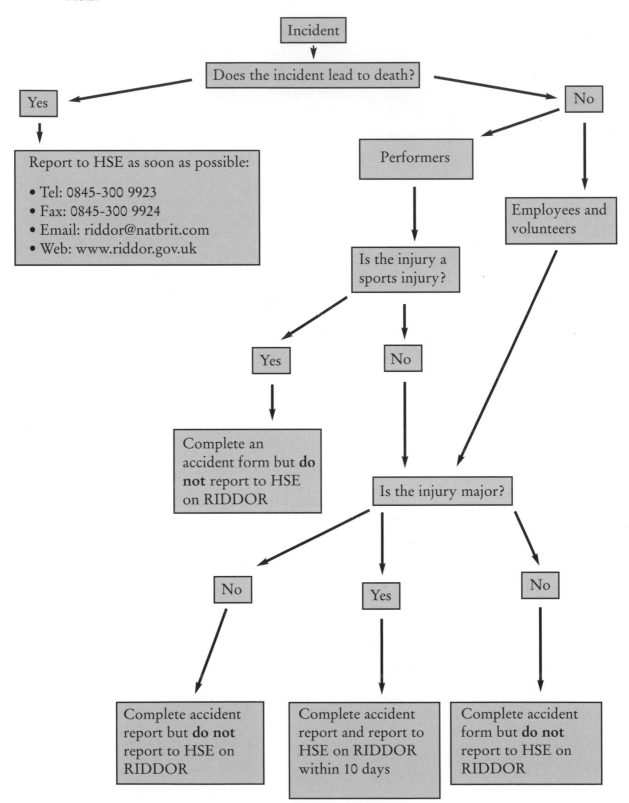

Figure 3: Reporting incidents to HSE

Appendix F

Criminal Records Bureau – Guidelines[1]

What is the Criminal Records Bureau?

The Criminal Records Bureau (CRB) has been set up by the Home Office to improve access to criminal record checks for employment-related and voluntary appointment purposes. In particular, it will provide protection for children and other vulnerable people against those who might wish to harm them.

Some sporting clubs/organisations already require police checks on those involved in sport with young people[2]. As recommended in Section 1.3 of this pack (see page 18), all sport and leisure providers should adopt this practice as part of an overall child protection policy.

Given the number of adults involved in either a paid or voluntary capacity in sporting clubs/organisations, obtaining, processing and storing the information will be a huge task. The aim of this appendix is to give guidance to sports clubs/organisations and national governing bodies on how to approach this.

When Should Someone be Checked?

The CRB provides a service to employers and volunteering groups in England and Wales[3] of all kinds called *Disclosure*. The employer will be able to use the Disclosure service to help establish whether a successful candidate has a background that might make them unsuitable for the position in question.

---

1   Adapted with kind permission from the Criminal Records Bureau and the Child Protection in Sport Unit.

2   While the information provided by the CRB is important in terms of recruitment and selection, organisations must recognise that this is only one of a much wider series of steps that need to be taken in order to create and sustain a safe environment for performers.

3   For information about Disclosure services in Scotland, telephone 0141-585 8495 or visit www.scro.police.uk, and in Northern Ireland, telephone 028-9052 0500 or visit www.dhsspsni.gov.uk

As well as using this service to check the background of new candidates, clubs/organisations should consider whether existing staff or volunteers should also be checked. This is especially important if an individual is being considered for a change in role that increases their contact with children.

This procedure will need to be implemented carefully within a club/organisation and may require amendments to current national governing body constitutions. It is important that the context for this action is fully communicated to all those involved in the sport and that issues of confidentiality are fully detailed. You will need to consider who within the national governing body will communicate this to staff and volunteers, and who will hold the information and make sure that this process complies with Data Protection Legislation.

One option that you may wish to consider is using a declaration as a means of implementing this procedure, such as the following statement:

*From (date), the governing body of (sport) adopted a child protection policy. This policy will ensure that (sport) takes all necessary steps to promote a safe atmosphere for all those children and young people involved in (sport). All those currently involved with (sport) with significant contact with children will be required to give an assurance that they have no previous criminal convictions that could put children at risk. This information is **strictly confidential** except for the legal obligation of reporting child abuse.*

The applicant initiates the Disclosure check and both the applicant and the employer receive copies of the Disclosure. You may wish to notify applicants of your intention to seek a Disclosure. A suggested statement to be included on all application forms is:

This post involves substantial access to children. As a club/organisation, we are committed to the welfare and protection of children. All applications to work with us in either a voluntary or paid capacity will involve a Criminal Records Bureau check.

 If a club/organisation knowingly appoints a person where a ban exists, they will be committing a criminal offence. Under the Protection of Children Act 1999, voluntary clubs/organisations are encouraged to report their concerns while registered children's clubs/organisations are obliged to report concerns.

Level of Disclosure

It will be up to each applying body to determine what is the appropriate level of Disclosure. The following table is designed to give guidance as to what level is appropriate. The CRB will provide three levels of Disclosure:

Level of Disclosure	What Checks Are Provided?	Who Would This Be Appropriate For?
Basic Disclosure	Unspent convictions.	Those working with the club in a position that brings them into indirect contact with children (eg fund-raisers, ticket–sellers).
Standard Disclosure	All convictions, cautions, reprimands or warnings plus information held by the Department of Health (DH) and Department for Education and Skills (DfES).	Those working directly with children who are **always** under the direct supervision of a senior official.
Enhanced Disclosure	All above checks plus an extra level of checking with local police force records.	Any individuals involved in a position offering significant direct contact with children (ie those in sole charge such as club coaches, teachers, team managers).

Please note: applications for the Standard and Enhanced Disclosures can only be made through a body that is registered with the CRB. The registered body must adhere to the CRB Code of Practice and ensure confidentiality. When a Disclosure is issued, a copy of this will be sent to both the registered body and the individual concerned. At some point in the future, any individual will be able to seek a Basic Disclosure for themselves.

More detailed information is available from the CRB and the Child Protection in Sport Unit (CPSU) at the following addresses:

Criminal Records Bureau PO Box 91 Liverpool L69 2UH Tel: 0870-90 90 811 Website: www.crb.gov.uk	**Child Protection in Sport Unit** NSPCC National Training Centre 3 Gilmour Close Beaumont Leys Leicester LE4 1EZ Tel: 0116-234 7278/7280 Fax: 0116-234 0464 Email: cpsu@nspcc.org.uk Website: www.thecpsu.org.uk

Appendix G

Further Reading

Books

Health and Safety Commission (2001) *Reducing At-work Road Traffic Incidents*. Sudbury: HSE Books. ISBN 0 7176 2239 8

Health and Safety Commission (1992) *Health and Safety Management in Higher and Further Education: guidance on inspection, monitoring and auditing*. Sudbury: HMSO/HSE Books. ISBN 0 11 886315 0

Health and Safety Executive (1996) *L73: A Guide to the Reporting of Injuries, Diseases and Dangerous Occurrences Regulations 1995*. Sudbury: HSE Books. ISBN 0 7176 1012 8

Health and Safety Executive (1997) *HSG 65: Successful Health and Safety Management*. Sudbury: HSE Books. ISBN 0 7176 1276 7

Kavanagh, C. and Hinde, A. (2001) *The Health and Safety Handbook for Voluntary and Community Organisations*. London Directory of Social Change in Association with Liverpool Occupational Health Partnership. ISBN 1 903991 01 3

Lester, G. (2002) *Protecting Children: a guide for sports people*. Leeds: Coachwise Solutions. ISBN 0 947850 70 3

sports coach UK (2003) *How to Coach Sports Safely*. Leeds: Coachwise Solutions. ISBN 1 902523 50 4

sports coach UK (2001) *Code of Conduct for Sports Coaches*. Leeds: Coachwise Solutions.

sports coach UK (2001) *Safe and Sound* (leaflet). Leeds: Coachwise Solutions.

St John Holt, A. (2003) *Principles of Health and Safety at Work* (6th edition). Leicester: IOSH Services Limited. ISBN 0 9013 5730 8

Appendix H

sports coach UK Contacts

sports coach UK

scUK works closely with sports governing bodies and other partners to provide a comprehensive service for coaches throughout the UK. This includes an extensive programme of workshops, which have proved valuable to coaches from all types of sports and every level of experience.

For further details of **scUK** workshops in your area, contact the **scUK** Business Support Centre (BSC).

sports coach UK Business Support Centre
Sports Development Centre
Loughborough University
Loughborough
Leicestershire LE11 3TU

Tel: 01509-226130
Fax: 01509-226134
Email: bsc@sportscoachuk.org

For further details on sports coaching in the UK, contact the **scUK** headquarters:

sports coach UK
114 Cardigan Road
Headingley
Leeds LS6 3BJ

Tel: 0113-274 4802
Fax: 0113-275 5019
Email: coaching@sportscoachuk.or
Website: www.sportscoachuk.org

Appendix I

Other Useful Contacts

Institute of Leisure and Amenities Management (ILAM)
Lower Basildon
Reading
RG8 9NE
Tel: 01491-874830

Institute of Sports and Recreation Management (ISRM)
Sir John Beckworth Centre for Sport
Loughborough University
Loughborough
Leicestershire
LE11 3TU
Tel: 01509-226474

Institution of Occupational Safety and Health (IOSH)
The Grange
Highfield Drive
Wigston
Leicestershire
LE18 1NN
Tel: 0116-257 3100

Health and Safety Information Centres

These are for personal callers who want to consult information held at these centres and are open Monday to Friday 09.00hrs – 17.00hrs:

Bootle Information Centre
HSE Information Centre
St Hugh's House
Stanley Precinct
Bootle
Merseyside
L20 3QY

London Information Centre
Rose Court
Southwark Bridge
London
SE1 9HS

Sheffield Information Centre
HSE Information Centres
Broad Lane
Sheffield
S3 7HQ
Fax: 0114-289 2333

The HSE also has 21 regional offices that may be contacted.

Every Local Authority will also have an Environmental Health Department to deal with health and safety issues.